First published in 2014
by Jessica Kingsley Publishers
116 Pentonville Road
London N1 9JB, UK
and
400 Market Street, Suite 400
Philadelphia, PA 19106, USA

www.jkp.com

Library of Congress Cataloging in Publication Data
A CIP catalog record for this book is available from the Library of Congress

British Library Cataloguing in Publication Data
A CIP catalogue record for this book is available from the British Library

ISBN 978 1 84905 935 0
eISBN 978 0 85700 740 7

Printed and bound in China

Ann Angel dedication
With love to Amanda, Nick, Joe and Stevi,
and with love to Beth, Suzanne and Bill

Marc Thomas dedication
For Jan, Joe and Zoe

of related interest

Different Like Me
My Book of Autism Heroes
Jennifer Elder
Illustrated by Marc Thomas and Jennifer Elder
ISBN 978 1 84310 815 3
eISBN 978 1 84642 466 3

The Mulberry Bird
An Adoption Story
Anne Braff Brodzinsky
Illustrated by Angela Marchetti
ISBN 978 1 84905 933 6
eISBN 978 0 85700 720 9

Can I tell you about Adoption?
A guide for friends, family and professionals
Anne Braff Brodzinsky
Illustrated by Rosy Salaman
ISBN 978 1 84905 942 8
eISBN 978 0 85700 759 9
Part of the Can I tell you about...? series

Contents

✎ Adopted Like Me ✎

If you're adopted like me, you're in the center of a loving family. I'm Max and my family includes my oldest sister Grace, my brother Nick and my little sister Ella. We're just like every other family with four kids, and a mom and a dad. We all live in a house with a big yard, with our mom and dad. We are a family. But our family is more complicated than some. We are a family through adoption. Each of my siblings has a set of birth parents who gave us life and we share adoptive parents who raise us. Adoption makes us a family.

We're *real* brothers and sisters who laugh, and play, sometimes bicker, and always love each other just the same as all brothers and sisters.

Some kids who are adopted are the only children in their families and some have brothers and sisters who are also their adoptive parents' birth children.

Some adoptions are closed, like mine, which means I don't know my birth parents even though I know some stories about their lives and my birth. I know about their history, which means I know about my own history. My birth parents loved me and gave me life but couldn't raise me. My adoptive parents wanted a big family full of children to love and so they arranged my adoption.

Some adoptions are open, like my sister Ella's. This means she shares letters and pictures with her birth mother.

But our family, the family we love and we're growing up in, is our forever and always family. Adoption is just the way we became a family. "This family," my mom always says, "is full of love." If you're adopted like me, you're in a forever family, a family full of love.

If you're adopted like me, we're not the only ones who are adopted either. Lots of famous people throughout history were adopted. Some people who have been adopted, or 'adoptees', are musicians, others are inventors, some are athletes and teachers. There are politicians, political activists, actors, scientists and even philosophers who are adopted. So if you're adopted like me, you can read about other adoptees whose lives show us we can grow up to be just about anything we want to be.

ೲ Moses ೮

Moses is one of the first adoption stories. According to the Bible, he was born in the thirteenth century BC, when Egypt's pharaoh feared a new leader might be rising up against him. The Pharaoh ordered all Hebrew baby boys, who were natives of Israel, to be drowned. To save her son, Moses' mother placed him in a basket in tall reeds along the Nile River. The Pharaoh's daughter discovered the basket. She was charmed and chose to raise the baby.

Fortunately, Moses' sister Miriam witnessed the discovery. She arranged for their mother to be his nurse. Moses grew up knowing his birth family, which included a brother named Aaron, but he was raised as a prince in the Pharaoh's home.

He learned to read and write many languages. One day he got into trouble when he tried to stop an Egyptian man from beating a Hebrew slave. Moses had to flee to Midian which is in Ethiopia where he married and had two sons.

Moses loved his life as a shepherd in a village. But he was a prophet, a man of divine wisdom. God sent an angel inside a burning bush to tell Moses to seek freedom for the Hebrews.

Moses wasn't sure this angel was really speaking God's will though. The angel turned Moses' staff into a serpent and then gave him leprosy and then cured it. Now Moses believed. God allowed Moses' brother Aaron to travel with him to help.

The Pharaoh refused to release the Hebrews to Moses so God sent plagues. These included turning water into blood killing all the fish, plagues of frogs, lice, flies and a disease of livestock. When these plagues didn't change the Pharaoh's mind, God sent more. A plague which brought death to firstborn children finally convinced the Pharaoh to allow the Hebrews to leave. This was called the Exodus.

Moses and the Hebrews escaped from Egypt, but the Pharaoh sent soldiers after them. They met at the Red Sea. God gave Moses power to part the sea. Before the soldiers could cross over, the sea closed again.

Moses and his people traveled for 40 years. To help his people, God gave Moses the Ten Commandments written on a stone tablet. Moses brought his people to a place called Canaan, which would be their home. He must have watched with great joy as they arrived.

❧ John Lennon ☙

John Lennon hardly knew his birth father, a merchant seaman who missed John's birth during an air raid in Liverpool, England, on October 9, 1940. When John was four, his parents split up. John's mother Julia asked her sister Mimi and Mimi's husband George to raise John, in a sort of informal adoption called "kinship care."

Julia moved a few blocks away and began a second family but she visited John, providing banjo and piano lessons and even giving him his first guitar.

As a schoolboy, John demonstrated creativity and loved to draw, but he was a prankster and a bit of a troublemaker. He didn't get very good grades but his teachers encouraged him to try art school. By the time he was 16, he had created a band called The Quarry Men. This was when John met Paul McCartney and the two formed a musical partnership that would change the face of rock and roll forever.

When John was 17, Julia died in an accident which devastated him. John used his music as an outlet for his grief. He focused on this and formed a new band called The Beatles with Paul McCartney. George Harrison came into the band and Ringo Starr was added in 1961. The four released the song "Love Me Do" in 1962 and quickly followed that with "Please Please Me."

The Beatles launched a British invasion of rock and roll when they brought a concert tour to the United States. Thousands of teen fans rushed stages, fainted and screamed for The Beatles. The four musicians gained even more fame when they made a nationally televised appearance on The Ed Sullivan Show on February 4, 1964. Although The Beatles reached mega-stardom, tensions between band members grew.

When John married the artist Yoko Ono, the new couple made international headlines with peace protests that included a "Bed-in" where they remained in bed while being filmed and interviewed, while singing "Give Peace a Chance." The couple's relationship created more tension within The Beatles. The group broke up in 1970.

John and Yoko formed the Plastic Ono Band. In 1971, John released his critically acclaimed album *Imagine*. Then, in 1980, John was killed outside his apartment by a mentally ill fan. The world mourned for this musician whose message is heard through the words of his songs as they call the world to "imagine all the people living life in peace."

℘ Marilyn Monroe ℘

A shy girl born on June 1, 1926 in Los Angeles, California, to a mother who suffered from mental illness, Norma Jean Baker never knew her father. Norma, who would grow up to become Marilyn Monroe, was placed in foster homes when her mother was ill in the hospital. Her mother's friend Grace and her boyfriend Doc took over guardianship, a legal decision similar to adoption where the courts appoint an adult or adults to raise a child when a birth parent is not able to do so. Norma struggled to read, a sign she suffered a learning disability called dyslexia, although she overcame this problem later. Of childhood, Norma said, "No one ever told me I was pretty when I was a little girl. All little girls should be told they're pretty, even if they aren't."

When she was 16 Norma married her boyfriend Jimmy Dougherty. After he was shipped to the South Pacific as a Merchant Marine to patrol the area and protect it from enemies, Norma worked at an ammunitions factory. She was discovered by a photographer there, and by the time Jimmy returned, she had a successful modeling career and had changed her name to Marilyn Monroe.

Divorced by 1946, Marilyn signed her first movie contract and dyed her hair blonde. After acting in *The Asphalt Jungle,* a famous film about a robbery, she gained a reputation as the breathy-voiced beauty.

Marilyn showed ability as a dramatic actress but her most memorable films were comedies such as *Gentlemen Prefer Blondes, Bus Stop* and *Some Like It Hot.* She received a Golden Globe award for *Some Like It Hot* in 1959. In 1962, in perhaps her most memorable appearance, Marilyn sang "Happy Birthday" to President John F. Kennedy.

Despite her physical beauty, Marilyn struggled. She wanted people to view her as intelligent and creative and attended literature and history classes at the University of California, Los Angeles. She read constantly and was often pictured in photos immersed in an open book. She also wrote poetry containing simple and clear ideas such as, "I think to love bravely is the best and accept—as much as one can bear." She is remembered as one of the most famous and recognizable female stars in Hollywood.

✆ Nelson Mandela ✇

Nelson Mandela was born on July 18, 1918 in Transkei, South Africa, a tribal village without running water or roads. He grew up to earn a Nobel Peace Prize in 1993 for his efforts to bring peace in his country through his work in the anti-apartheid movement. This was a movement in Africa to end racial segregation, which was created by laws that made it illegal for black people to vote and kept white and black people from working or living together.

His father, a tribal leader, gave Nelson the name Rolihlahla which can be translated to mean "pulling the branch of a tree." As a child, he lived in a hut where the family cooked locally harvested food outdoors. He was given the name Nelson by his school teacher on his first day of school. In those days it was common for children to be given English names if they did not already have one.

When he was nine, Nelson's father died. He was adopted by Chief Jongintaba Dalindyebo, the acting King of the Thembu people, and sent to his village to live. The King groomed Nelson for leadership as counselor to other chiefs and educated him in the history of Africa. When the King attempted to arrange his marriage, Nelson ran away to Johannesburg. Here, Nelson first experienced what black life was like for urban South Africans and it set him on a path to defy unjust laws in his country. In 1944, he helped to form the African National Congress (ANC) Youth League. This group called for protests that included civil disobedience and strikes in which people stopped providing work and services to protest the laws that forced them to live in a segregated country. His devotion to equality and willingness to protest drew the attention of the government and politicians who didn't want him to have power.

He was often arrested and sent to prison, eventually spending a total of 27 years in prison, only being freed at the age of 71 in 1990. Nelson refused to give up his dream of a free Africa, a country where everyone—not just white people—had the right to vote, so he continued to lead his people toward this. He was elected President of South Africa in 1994 and served until 1999.

In 1996, Nelson Mandela achieved his dream of equality for all South Africans when he signed the new South African Constitution which guaranteed equal rights for all, freedom of expression and a range of other freedoms. Nelson retired from public life in June 2004 at the age of 85. He will always be remembered as a symbol of freedom for all.

✂ Steve Jobs ✂

It's hard to picture a world before cell phones or personal computers, where the iPad, iPod and iTunes have yet to be imagined. Steve Jobs was born on February 24, 1955, before this technology had been invented, and he was to play a big part in creating it. The birth son of two university students, Steve was an infant when he was adopted by Clara, an accountant, and Paul Jobs, a Coast Guard veteran and mechanic. The family lived in California, on the West Coast of the United States. While Steve was growing up, televisions were boxy and large, and telephones required cords. Video games didn't even exist yet.

Steve would explore the workings of electronic things alongside his dad in the family's garage. Steve showed a real aptitude for taking apart mechanical things and putting them together. School frustrated him. He was known for pulling so many pranks that his fourth grade teacher tried to bribe him to study.

Steve chose Reed College in Portland, Oregon after high school but dropped out after one semester. After that, he attended classes, picking and choosing only those that engaged his innovative and creative mind. While sitting in a calligraphy class, learning artistic and elegant handwriting, he discovered he liked to design different fonts for the alphabet. By 1974, he was applying this knowledge as a video game designer.

Steve found it difficult to settle into any single thing and so he left his job and traveled the Asian continent, spending time in India thinking about life and spiritual matters and undertaking strict vegan dietary habits. In 1976, he returned to California. It was around this time that Steve learned his birth parents had married briefly and he had a sister, novelist Mona Simpson. The two met and became friends. It was about the same time that Steve sold his Volkswagon bus and used the profits to create Apple Computers in the Jobs' family garage.

Steve was about to revolutionize the computer industry, designing computers that were smaller, and more easily operated. Nothing like his computer ideas had been created yet. Steve created Pixar industries to make movies such as *Toy Story, Cars* and *Finding Nemo* and developed innovative methods of using computers for movie animation. His computer design ideas made personal computers accessible to the world. Today, most of Steve's innovations, including iPads and iPods, can be found in most homes.

John James Audubon

John James Audubon's birth mother was a servant girl of mixed French and Spanish ancestry. She lived in Santo Domingo, a French colony of the Dominican Republic located in the Caribbean region. John's mother died shortly after his birth on April 26, 1785. Although she and John's father had a baby together, they never got married. After John's mother died his father married another lady—she was John's step-mother. John's father sent him and his half-sister, who shared the same birth mother as him, to live with her in France. She and John's father legally adopted him and his half-sister in 1794.

John's father hoped to groom his son into a good businessman, but John wanted nothing to do with business or with formal education. His father arranged for tutoring in mathematics, drawing, music and fencing or swordfighting. Although he demonstrated a real talent for drawing, John preferred the outdoors to the classroom. In an effort to encourage John to take his studies a bit more seriously, John's father sent him to Paris for a short while to study art. John enjoyed drawing but he disliked the stuffiness of studying art in college and returned home.

His parents sent John to a family farm in Pittsburgh, Pennsylvania hoping the change would encourage John to consider life as a businessman.

Although the move to a new continent didn't encourage John to take his studies any more seriously, he took great pleasure in hunting, fishing and drawing. He was so intent on capturing the natural poses of birds that he developed a wiring system to pose freshly dead birds. In doing so, he was able to capture the natural beauty of birds in nature.

Turning his talent to profit, John made crayon drawings of people and charged $5 per portrait while his wife helped support their growing family as a teacher in a girl's school. He also became a taxidermist but he never lost his real passion to draw birds and wildlife in nature. Then, one day, John hit on a brilliant idea. He would find a publisher for his bird pictures and bind them in a book. It took about 11 years, but *Birds of America* was published in 1827, making the artist a famous naturalist whose works are still regarded as brilliant representations of the environment.

ℬ Aristotle ℭ

Aristotle, who was born about 384 BC in Greece, would grow up to become a man who loved wisdom. As one of history's greatest philosophers, he developed a system called "rational argument" for studying elements of humanity, such as knowledge, language and reason.

His father, a doctor for the king of Macedonia in a region of Greece, died when Aristotle was only a young boy. His mother also died when he was young. Aristotle was raised by his older sister Arimnetse and her husband, Proxenus of Atarneus. The couple noticed the way the young boy questioned everything from math to biology and even politics. They sent him to Athens to study at the philosopher Plato's academy, a school that encouraged students to question ideas and explore all of life. Aristotle investigated and studied everything he could while remaining at the academy for about 20 years. But Plato thought Aristotle took questioning too far when he questioned Plato's teaching. Aristotle, who had thought he would become the academy's next director after Plato's death, didn't get the job.

Aristotle returned to Macedonia, married and had a daughter, Phythias. For a while, Aristotle taught Alexander the Great, one of the greatest military geniuses of all time. Then Aristotle returned to Athens and opened his own academy called the Lyceum. Here students studied math, science, politics and philosophy. Aristotle would often walk around the school grounds teaching and observing his surroundings. His eager students followed. From him, they learned, "Excellence…is not an act, but a habit."

Aristotle's wife died during his first year at the Lyceum. He later adopted a son, Nichomachus. He continued to question everything. Aristotle wrote over 200 works but only 31 still circulate—the others have been lost over the years. His research topics included efforts to classify animals into red-blooded "vertebrates" and bloodless "cephalopods," and marine biology. He also researched earth science, which studies how earth's systems work, and meteorology, which studies the atmosphere and weather. He described the water cycle in which rain falls, collects and then evaporates to be collected once again into rain clouds.

Aristotle also discovered hibernation, worker bees, that birds have territories and migration of animals and fishes. His theories, along with Plato's, are the foundation of most of the Western world's thinking. He was loved as a teacher and philosopher who practiced and believed, "All men by nature desire to know."

❧ George Washington Carver ☙

George Washington Carver was never certain of his birthday. An African-American, he was born into slavery, a system in which people are bought and sold to work. He was born around 1864 on a Missouri cotton plantation owned by Moses Carver and his wife Susan. This was during the Civil War, a war fought between American states over freedom for the slaves.

George's father Giles, who died in an accident before his birth, and his mother Mary were also slaves. When George was one week old he, a sister and his mother were stolen by raiders. The Carvers found George and brought him back home, but they never found the others. They raised George and a brother in their home. Susan taught them there because no local schools would allow black students. Always curious, George's interest in plants earned him the nickname the "Plant Doctor." He was encouraged to pursue more education.

George traveled ten miles each way to a school for black children, earning his high school diploma from Minneapolis High School in Kansas. An excellent student, he was accepted into Highland College in Kansas, but then turned away because he was black. This didn't dissuade George from learning. He took advantage of the Homestead Act, a program where the government granted free land for farming, to experiment with plant biology, before attending Simpson College in Iowa to study art. His professors recognized his skills and encouraged him to study botany at the much larger Iowa State College.

George became the first black student at Iowa State. After earning a degree, he turned to teaching and studying at the first college for African-Americans, Tuskegee Institute. George devoted his study to agriculture and trained students on crop rotation methods that encourage planting different crops each year or leaving fields unplanted so that important minerals aren't stripped from the soil. Many of the farmers he helped were also freed slaves. When they couldn't get to George, he developed a school on wheels, the "Jesup Wagon"— so-called because a New York financier named Morris K. Jessup provided the money for it.

George developed new uses for traditional crops such as sweet potatoes, pecans, soybeans and peanuts, creating paint and plastic, dyes and gasoline from them. He became an internationally famous scientist and role model. He believed every person should work to make the world better, saying, "No individual has any right to come into the world and go out of it without leaving behind him distinct and legitimate reasons for having passed through it."

ᕲ Fatima Whitbread ᕱ

On March 3, 1961 Fatima Whitbread was born in Stoke Newington, London. Shortly after her birth, her mother abandoned her in a flat. She was rescued by the police.

Fatima struggled in care homes for 14 years before a teacher and coach at her school, Margaret Whitbread, recognized her potential. She and her husband adopted Fatima, and Margaret, a former javelin thrower and coach, began training her new daughter in the sport. Under her mother's coaching Fatima became European Junior Champion in 1979. She reached the highest levels with this sport and competed in the Olympics. She and her teammate Tessa Sanderson dominated in competitions throughout the 1980s. Much to Fatima's annoyance, Tessa won the gold while Fatima won the Olympic bronze medal in Los Angeles, California, when the 1984 Olympics was hosted by the United States. Fatima followed this up with a silver medal in Seoul, Korea in 1988. The rivalry between Fatima and Tessa was intense and occasionally became bitter although the two respected one another for their competitive spirits.

In 1986, Fatima won the javelin throwing world record. Within a year she was named BBC Sports Personality of the year and in 1988 she was named World Champion. She retired from javelin competition in 1992 because of a chronic shoulder injury. Fatima married and had one son. She recently ventured back into the public eye when she joined the television cast of a reality TV show.

Fatima hasn't forgotten what it's like to be in foster care. As an ambassador for the Foster Network, an organization that campaigns to improve foster care and gives support and advice to its members, she shares the hope that children in care homes today can find loving parents through adoption, just as she found her family and love with the Whitbreads. She said, "Now I feel a moral obligation to try to correct some of the wrongs for other children."

❧ Bo Diddley ❧

Named Ellas Otha Bates, the boy who would grow up known for bringing a new beat to rock and roll, was born on December 30, 1928 in Mississippi. He was adopted by his mother's cousin and raised in south-side Chicago. As a young boy, he had an ear for music and took up trombone and violin. While playing in his Baptist church's orchestra, Ellas also discovered the pulsing, powerful beat of music, and soon added guitar to his list of accomplishments. All that music made people think Ellas had a knack for working with instruments so they sent him to a vocational school to learn how to make violins and guitars. But Ellas wanted to play.

He changed his name to Bo Diddley which he felt more fitting for a rock and roll performer. This name may have originated from a one-stringed instrument called the Diddley Bow. Bo claimed there was another singer he admired who had the name first. Others claim Bo named himself after a boxing champion.

Bo Diddley became most famous for the "Bo Diddley" beat, originally the "hambone," a technique used by street performers who played a beat by slapping their arms and legs, chests and cheeks while chanting rhyming lyrics.

During the late 1950s, Bo's recordings reached the Top Forty on music charts with his song "Pretty Things" and remained there with "Who Do You Love" and "Before You Accuse Me." But then people stopped listening to his music so much, as they were listening to newer styles of rock and roll.

Then in 1979, the punk rock band The Clash introduced Bo's music to a new generation of teen musicians. Finally, when Bo was in his fifties, in 1996, he was recognized by the Rock and Roll Hall of Fame as a pioneering force in music. He received a Lifetime Achievement Award in 1996 from the Rhythm and Blues Foundation. Before dying of a heart attack in 2008, Bo had influenced many generations of musicians, including the Rolling Stones and Bruce Springstein, to explore music's heavy beats. His influence continues to be felt in rock, blues and hip hop.

໙ Edgar Allan Poe ໕

Known for writing horror stories and poetry, Edgar Allan Poe is the father of the modern detective story. Born to traveling actors on January 19, 1809, Edgar and his siblings hardly knew their parents. His father left. His mother died when he was three, and Edgar was separated from his brother and sister. He was adopted and raised by a successful tobacco merchant, John Allan, and his wife Frances. They encouraged Edgar to be a businessman. But Edgar's hero had always been British poet Lord Byron, considered one of the greatest poets ever and who was one of the leaders of the Romantic Movement. His long poems were often about romantic relationships.

Edgar wanted to write. When John attempted to teach his son about business, Edgar turned the business papers over to pen his poems.

A good student, Edgar left his home to enroll in the University of Virginia. He lived on a small allowance from John.

Edgar had a good relationship with Frances, but his father's efforts to teach him about finances made him angry. Edgar decided to prove he could earn a living as a poet. At 18, he published his first book, *Tamerlane*. Then he joined the US Army.

Edgar returned to Virginia after Frances died. He and his father made peace long enough for John to help him gain an appointment at one of the United States' most respected officer training programs at West Point Academy. Meanwhile, Edgar was determined to prove he was a writer, not an officer. After publishing two more books of poetry, he decided to leave the Academy and pursue writing.

Edgar's writing career wasn't immediately successful so his birth father's sister Maria took him in for a while. He started to write short stories to try to make some money and then he was hired, at 27, by a newspaper called the *Southern Literary Messenger*. Now that he was employed, Edgar invited Maria and her 13-year-old daughter to live with him in Richmond, Virginia.

The publication of his poem, "The Raven," in 1896 earned such a following that Edgar's lectures started to fill halls. He spent most of the rest of his life traveling the country lecturing and trying to raise funds for a new magazine.

Tashunca-uitco (Crazy Horse)

Crazy Horse's mother and father, both members of the Native American Soioux tribe, a village of people who shared customs and beliefs, named him Tashunca-uitco at his birth around 1840. Because he was born with a head of curly hair his people also called him Curly as a child. He was an adolescent when he was adopted and trained to be a warrior by High Back Bone, a Sioux warrior. Even as young as 13, Crazy Horse was legendary, unafraid to steal horses from members of a rival tribe of Crow Indians. Before he was 20, he was leading war parties against other tribes and American settlers who threatened his tribe's native way of life.

As an adult, he was recognized by his people as a great leader and warrior, a visionary who protected the tribal way of life, which included the belief that no one could own land but that all of nature should be shared and respected. But this was a time when European settlers wanted land to farm and fought the Native Americans to gain it. They tried to confine all members of all tribes to reservations with treaties or written documents that traded land for money and furs, food and other living necessities. Crazy Horse didn't trust the settlers or these treaties and became a loner who refused to bend against his foes.

This brave warrior refused to sign his name to any document or to allow his photograph to be taken by the settlers. He also refused to be confined to the reservations, which were usually the least desirable lands, and he became a leader of the resistance against American settlers' efforts to restrict him. In 1876, he led his warriors to victory in the famous battle against the US Army under Colonel George Custer at the Battle of Little Big Horn. But Crazy Horse was pursued for five years. As food supplies grew short, his warriors abandoned him and, finally, Crazy Horse surrendered at Red Cloud.

When his wife grew sick on the reservation, Crazy Horse again demonstrated his courage and independence. He left the reservation without permission to take his wife to her parents. General George Crook, who feared he would return to battle, ordered his arrest. While being led to a guardhouse, Crazy Horse began to struggle and one of the soldiers ran him through with a bayonet, a blade attached to a gun, which killed him. Even years after his death, he was praised for his vision of freedom for his people and their way of life.

ಶಿ J.R.R. Tolkien ಞ

Although he is known throughout the world as the writer of *The Hobbit,* a tale of imaginary little people living in the land of Middle Earth, and *The Lord of the Rings* trilogy, J.R.R. Tolkien was also a language scholar of Old and Middle English.

Born John Ronald Reuel Tolkien on January 3, 1892, Ronald remembered little of his early childhood in South Africa. That ended shortly after he turned four when Ronald's father died and his mother returned to their home in England to raise Ronald and his younger brother Hilary. Here, details of growing up in a house bounded by a railway were fixed in his memory. The family's genteel poverty became rich experience as Ronald imagined magical distant lands.

When he was 12, Ronald and his brother became orphaned when their mother died of complications from diabetes. Penniless and rejected by relatives who disapproved of their Catholic faith, a Christian religion that was stricter than their own Protestant Christianity, the boys were adopted by an aunt. She had a Catholic priest, Father Francis Morgan, to educate them. Ronald had already mastered Latin and Greek and demonstrated such ability to learn languages that he made up some words and languages of his own while also learning Finnish and ancient Gothic languages.

At 16, Ronald developed a liking for Edith Bratt who was 19. When Father Morgan learned of this, he banned Ronald from seeing her for three years. Obeying, Ronald registered at Exeter College, part of Oxford University. He specialized in modern and ancient German languages.

World War I broke out about the same time Ronald and Edith were able to renew their relationship. Ronald enlisted in the military and married his love. After serving in the military, Ronald returned to Oxford to teach with his young family. He wrote short Father Christmas stories for his children and often joined a group of friends who nicknamed themselves "The Inklings" for evenings of storytelling at a local pub.

It was a good life that included teaching university students and grading exams. One day, Ronald came across an empty page in a student's exam book and scribbled on the page, "In a hole in the ground there lived a hobbit." This simple thought eventually led him to write his first book, *The Hobbit*, and then the classic series of three books about hobbits, humans, trolls, dwarves and elves, *The Lord of the Rings*. His books have been read by millions and made into popular movies.

Princess Xianzi of the Qing Dynasty

For almost 200 years, from 1644 to 1911, the Qing Dynasty practiced adopting children between members of the imperial family to make sure there was a new emperor or empress if a leader died without having children. Princess Xianzi, born in 1907, was one of the last princesses adopted during the reign of this dynasty. The fourteenth birth daughter of Prince Zhan Ji, who had 21 sons and 17 daughters, she and a birth brother were adopted in 1913 by a Japanese military advisor, Naniwa Kawashima.

The princess attended school in Tokyo and learned judo and fencing. Her father wanted her to marry a prince so she did, but she soon ran away from her marriage and became a friend of the Empress of the Forbidden City, a walled section of China's capital city that enclosed the imperial palace and government buildings.

Xianzi, who was also known as Kawashima Yoshiko, longed to be a liberated woman. She joined a Japanese colony in Shanghai, Yoshiko and began dressing in riding breeches and boots. As an intelligence agent, Xianzi, who had many connections to important people, convinced the last Chinese emperor, Pu Yi, to serve as the chosen ruler of Manchuria so that she could gain government information. Her ability to gather information between the Japanese and Chinese, at a time when the Japanese military occupied and controlled parts of China, increased her fortunes greatly and allowed her to live life the way she chose.

ᔒ Jean-Jacques Rousseau ᔓ

Jean-Jacques Rousseau, the son of a well-educated watchmaker from Geneva, Switzerland, lost his mother to a fever only days after his birth on June 17, 1712. His father's sister Suzanne helped raise Jean and his older brother. Their home was filled with music and stories and Jean often read aloud in his father's workshop while his father worked.

When Jean was ten, his father was caught trespassing and had to flee town to avoid prosecution. Jean and his brother were left in the care of an uncle, in a sort of informal adoption called "kinship care."

The uncle packed the boys off to live with a minister. The minister followed a religion called Calvinism, which emphasizes the rule of God over all things. Under the minister's teaching and guidance, Jean learned math and drawing and developed such strong Christian beliefs he considered becoming a minister. But Jean's uncle, who was still his legal guardian, believed Jean needed work skills so he apprenticed Jean to people working in trades like printing and engraving.

At 15, after a three-year apprenticeship to an engraver who beat him, Jean ran away. Guided by his spiritual upbringing, he sought the protection of a priest who followed a different type of religion, called Catholicism. The priest helped him become the secretary of a noblewoman, Françoise-Louise de Warens, who encouraged Jean to become Catholic and arranged music lessons.

Jean's interest in music led him to travel through Europe and finally to settle in Paris. His curiosity about humanity and spirituality was so strong, it led him into discussions and arguments. He finally turned to writing to put his ideas into a book, *Discourse on the Arts and Sciences*. He wrote, "Man is born free, and he is everywhere in chains." He explained that, although humans are naturally good, they became corrupt and spoiled by society. He believed laws should shape the way we live together. His writing helped bring about the Age of Enlightenment, which was a time when people learned many new things about science and changed how they thought about God and the world around them. His writing also helped to change the laws which decide how people live together.

He also wrote about education. Jean believed that girls should be free to think and work, but in support of their future husbands. Overall, he emphasized friendships and self-sacrifice in the interest of others. He wrote, "All that we lack at birth, all that we need when we come to man's estate, is the gift of education." He believed, "The noblest work in education is to make a reasoning man."

❧ Dave Thomas ☙

David Thomas never knew his birth mother. He was adopted six weeks after his birth on July 2, 1932. Sadly, his adoptive mother died when he was only five, but his adoptive father was still there to look after him. Dave spent his early years traveling from state to state while his dad sought work. Dave learned to look forward to long summer days staying at his grandmother Minnie Sinclair's home in Michigan. Under her guidance, he learned to treat people well and do the right things, and he learned important things about quality and service. Years after he became a successful owner of the Wendy's Hamburgers chain, he credited his grandmother with teaching him the qualities he needed to run this successful business.

Dave's very first job was in a restaurant as a counterman. He loved the business and dropped out of school at 15 to work fulltime at the Hobby House restaurant. When his father announced another move, Dave decided to stay at the Hobby House and moved into the local YMCA residences. After he met Colonel Sanders, the founder of Kentucky Fried Chicken (KFC), he worked at four KFC restaurants that weren't making very much money. He did so well that when he sold them back to KFC, he became a millionaire at age 35.

On November 15, 1969 he achieved the dream of his childhood when he opened his first Wendy's Old Fashioned Hamburgers restaurant in Columbus, Ohio. He named the restaurant after one of his daughters. Unlike other fast food restaurants, he carpeted and decorated it to feel like dining in a comfortable home. Dave served freshly made hamburgers hot off the grill, while other restaurants grilled the food ahead of time and kept it warm in trays. His hamburgers were square rather than round and Dave liked to say, "We don't cut corners!"

Despite his success, the lack of a high school diploma bothered Dave and so, at 60, he returned to school at Coconut Creek High School in Florida where he was named "Most Likely to Succeed" at his graduation in 1993.

Dave believed in giving back and felt a special connection to children waiting to be adopted. He said every child should have a loving family. In 1990, he was named to serve on the White House Initiative on Adoption which increased the country's awareness of children in need of adoption. Two years later, he established the Dave Thomas Foundation for Adoption, a public charity with one primary goal: to help every child in foster care find a permanent, loving family. He often said his two legacies were Wendy's and the Dave Thomas Foundation and that his greatest accomplishment in life was his wife Lorraine, his children and his grandchildren.

❧ Sarah Saffian ❧

Sarah Saffian's birth parents placed her for adoption when she was an infant. Her childhood was one in which she always felt confident and well-loved even though her adoptive mom died when she was only six. Her father remarried and her parents gave birth to two more children. Sarah, now one of three siblings, grew up to become a writer.

One morning as she was leaving for work her phone rang. When she picked it up, she heard the voice of her birth mother on the other end of the phone. Sarah learned that her birth parents had married each other and given birth to three additional siblings. She discovered that she immediately felt deeply protective of everyone—this newly discovered birth mother, her adoptive parents, her siblings—but she also felt as if the world spun crazily and she was overwhelmed.

After that phone call, Sarah wasn't sure what to do. So she continued her day as if nothing had changed. But she couldn't concentrate and she couldn't focus. She finally called her adoptive dad and broke down in tears. He told her to come home.

Sarah rushed into his comforting arms when he opened the door and she was flooded with relief. She wrote about that day in her book *Ithaka,* a daughter's memoir about being found. "Relief flowed through me as we hugged and I breathed in his warm, fatherly smell of soap and coffee and cigarettes."

Sarah's birth father called her the following week, and she asked him to slow down. She wasn't ready for the phone calls or pictures and she certainly wasn't ready to meet them face to face. She asked that they exchange letters instead.

Confronted with the reality of a family of people connected to her by birth, the young writer needed to reconsider her identity as an adoptee and as a birth child. As letters were exchanged and Sarah learned about the parents who had originally named her Susan, she struggled to figure her life out. After three years of exchanging letters and photos, Sarah was ready to meet the parents of her birth. In the end, she wrote *Ithaka* in the hope that her experience would offer insight to adoptees, birth parents and adoptive parents alike, and that her story, with its focus on identity and belonging, would also be interesting to readers who might not have experienced adoption in their families.

ഌ Arn Chorn-Pond ജ

Arn Chorn, born into a family of musicians, was only nine when he and his family were captured by the Khmer Rouge, a violent political group. This group, led by the dictator Pol Pot, took control of Cambodia in 1975. Many people were killed and Arn witnessed terrible suffering. He survived by volunteering to play music for the soldiers.

When Vietnamese soldiers invaded Cambodia in 1979, Arn escaped, walking for weeks to reach a refugee camp. In 1980, a Lutheran minister, Peter Pond, who helped the refugees and taught them about his Christian beliefs, befriended the teenager, adopted him and brought him to the United States.

Because of his father's encouragement, Arn decided to dedicate his life to ending the suffering of children hurt by this war. After graduating from a university with a degree, Arn worked through an organization that works with refugees, called the Religious Task Force, to create the charity Children of War, an organization he runs to help children and young adults in refugee camps. By bringing United States' teens together with children surviving war, Arn brings positive change. He has testified before the United Nations for Amnesty International, an organization that works for human rights, working to prevent the return of war and human rights violations.

When he returned to Cambodia to help rebuild the country, Arn found the musicians of his land destitute and living on the streets. Arn formed the Cambodia Masters Performers Project. This program unites traditional and classical Cambodian musicians with the country's children and keeps their music alive. The organization's name has changed to Cambodian Living Arts.

Arn's story was captured in the award-winning biographical novel *Never Fall Down,* written by Patricia McCormick. He has received the Reebok Human Rights Award, the Anne Frank Memorial Award, the Kohl Foundation International Peace Prize and two universities have honored him with the highest level of degree by awarding him honorary doctorates for peace and humanitarian service and providing help for refugees. This talented musician, who plays the flute and has made CDs and DVDs with musicians from his country, travels the world spreading his message of peace to young people. He says his greatest pleasure is to find young musicians and nurture them to reclaim their homeland's legacy. "I myself would like to become a man of peace, if I can," he says. "I don't want any child to go through what I went through."

Langston Hughes

Shortly after poet Langston Hughes was born on February 1, 1902 in Joplin, Missouri, his parents divorced. His mother struggled to take care of him so his grandmother took over raising the quiet young boy who found solace in books. Langston's grandmother, a vivid storyteller, encouraged his love of literature and made him realize education was important.

In 1914, when he was 12, Langston returned to live with his mother and her new husband. A good student who excelled in school, Langston wrote his first poem when he was only in eighth grade. Although the family moved around a lot to find work, he was popular with his classmates who voted him class poet and editor of the high school yearbook during his senior year at Central High School in Cleveland, Ohio.

Langston settled in Harlem, New York for a time from 1921. The Harlem Renaissance was happening—a period of great cultural development for African-American literature, music, theater, art and politics. Langston would often sit in clubs listening to blues while he wrote poetry. He was one of the first poets to use the sounds of jazz to depict African-American themes.

He also earned his way onto ships that traveled the world, visiting Mexico, Europe and Africa. He wrote poetry in Paris and worked as a busboy in Washington, DC, where he met poet Vachel Lindsay who used his influence to bring Langston's poetry to the attention of publishers. His poem "The Weary Blues" won first prize in a magazine contest before being added to his collection, which was also called *The Weary Blues*, in 1926. At this time Langston also received a scholarship to study at Lincoln University in Pennsylvania, where his poetry was recognized by his teachers.

With the successful publication of his novel *Not Without Laughter* in 1929, Langston became one of the first African-Americans to earn a living as a writer. He went on to write books, plays, Broadway music lyrics, essays and an autobiography.

After Langston died on May 22, 1967, his ashes were buried in Harlem beneath the entrance of the Arthur Schomburg Center for Research in Black Culture. The spot is marked with a line from his poem "The Negro Speaks of Rivers." It reads, "My soul has grown deep like the rivers."

ɞ Adopted Like Me ᴄʀ

Wow, those people made a big difference in the world! Whether they were legally adopted, raised by "guardians," or lived with relatives in "kinship care," their families loved them and tried to help them achieve their dreams. Their dreams led them to become artists, musicians, writers, philosophers and scientists. Some became actors and some became teachers, and social and political leaders.

I already have lots of dreams. I like to share them with my family and they encourage me to work to make those dreams come true. Then I'll decide what I'm going to do with my life, and how I can make a difference in the world…just like all the great people before me.